THE LIGHT OF OUR LAST STAR

Also by Angelina Schreiber:

My State of Felicity
dear inner child
A Million Letters to Write

The Light of
Our Last Star

Angelina Schreiber

Bibliografische Information der Deutschen Nationalbibliothek: Die Deutsche Nationalbibliothek verzeichnet diese Publikation in der Deutschen Nationalbibliografie; detaillierte bibliografische Daten sind im Internet über http://dnb.dnb.de abrufbar.

Verlag: BoD · Books on Demand GmbH, Überseering 33, 22297 Hamburg, bod@bod.de
Druck: Libri Plureos GmbH, Friedensallee 273, 22763 Hamburg
ISBN: 978-3-8192-4707-1

To what was real, even if it didn't last,
and to the light I carry because of it.

⋆₀°☆ **Chapter 1: First Light** ☆°₀⋆

"They say the first star is the bravest,
the one that dares to shine before the others catch on."

You were not a spark.
You were not a storm.
You were something quieter, the slow unfolding of light at
dusk.
The kind of light that doesn't shout, just... stays.

I don't remember what you wore that first time.
I don't remember the exact words you said.
But I remember the way the air changed when you walked
into the room.
Like the universe paused, just for a moment, and tilted
slightly in your direction.

We didn't collide.
We aligned.
Two people orbiting a life they hadn't imagined yet.

I had spent years being the I-can-do-it-on-my-own girl.
Not because I wanted to be, but because I didn't know there
was another way.
And then you,
you offered your hand when I stood up.
You filled my plate before your own.
You poured my wine and didn't make a show of it.
You just... did it.
Like love was meant to be practical, too.
Like safety could live in the smallest things.

You didn't ask me to soften.
But I did.
Without even noticing.
We started with late-night conversations that stretched across the stars.
I told you about the way I used to sit by my window as a child and look for constellations.
You told me you always liked the moon more than the sun.
You said the moon doesn't demand attention, she just reflects what she's given.
I didn't know then how much that would matter later.

I wrote that your eyes were the poem I never intended to write.
And it was true.
You looked at me like I was something worth reading slowly.
Like I was not just a pretty sentence, but a story.
We talked about music, and I joked that I had a playlist for every mood.
You laughed and said, *"Make one for me someday."*
I already had.

You never called me too much.
Not once.
You listened when I rambled.
You laughed when I got dramatic.
You remembered the titles of the poems I was too shy to read aloud.
You saw all of me, the chaos and the calm, and you stayed.

I don't know when it started.
But I remember lying in your arms one night, my head on your chest, listening to the sound of your heartbeat like it was

music made just for me.

And I remember thinking, *"I want to freeze this moment. I want to make time stop, just for a second, just long enough to memorize how this feels."*

For the first time in my life, I wasn't waiting for the other shoe to drop.
I wasn't bracing for goodbye.
I was just there.
With you.
Safe.
Still.
Seen.

You made my heart so happy it spilled out of me.
In texts I almost didn't send.
In poems I scribbled on napkins.
In little notes I left behind when you weren't looking.
You made love feel like light, not burning, but warm.

And suddenly, I was falling.
Not tripping, not crashing,
just falling.
Softly.
Fully.
Like gravity had finally decided to be kind.

I was falling into the small kisses you gave me.
Each one a spark, each one a gentle flame.
I was falling into your hands, the way they held me like something rare.
Like something you didn't want to break.

I was falling into your laughter, your quiet steadiness, your
bad jokes.
I was falling into the space you carved out for me.
Like a star falling into orbit.
Like I had been searching for your pull all along.

You made me believe in happy poems again.
In stories that don't end in heartbreak.
In a love that didn't ache, but glowed.

You didn't rescue me.
You didn't fix me.
You simply stood beside me and said,
"Even your shadows are beautiful."

And maybe that was the spark.
The first light.
The beginning of everything.

⋆₀°☆ **Chapter 2: Gravity** ☆°₀⋆

"Some stars don't explode.
They settle,
burning steadily, softly,
becoming the quiet center
of someone's world."

I didn't fall all at once.
I let go slowly.
Like a sunflower turning to face the sun, unsure, at first, if it was safe to bloom.
Like the way the sky fades from night into morning,
not with fanfare, but with stillness.
A soft unveiling.

You didn't rush me.
You didn't pull.
You just stayed, patient, warm, a kind of gravity I didn't know I was already circling.

There were no grand confessions.
Just small things.
Your hand brushing mine while we walked through town.
Your hoodie left behind on my chair.
The way you said my name like it was something worth saying softly.
The way my face fit perfectly in your hands, like it was always meant to rest there.

You were never loud.
There were no fireworks, no chaos.
Just this gentle pull.
A stillness that said, *you don't have to run anymore.*

Some nights, we didn't speak at all.
You'd rest your head in my lap, eyes closed, breathing slow.
And I'd run my fingers through your hair like it was the only
prayer I knew.
We didn't need words.
We had silence.
And in that silence, something sacred grew.

I was used to fighting for love,
used to earning space, proving my worth.
But with you, it just was.
Steady.
Uncomplicated.
Like my heart had finally found solid ground.

With you, I stopped flinching at kindness.
Stopped preparing for disappointment.
You watered the parts of me I forgot to tend to.
And when I bloomed,
you didn't take credit.
You just smiled, proud, quiet, whole.

I started writing happy poems again.
Lines that didn't ache, but lifted.
Verses that breathed in soft syllables.
You made joy feel like ink.
You made hope sound like a song I could hum again.
You made me fall in love with words that glowed instead of
bled.

And slowly, without even realizing it,
I let you see the parts of me that had always felt too heavy for
anyone else to hold.
My tangled thoughts. My soft spots. The chapters I hadn't

read aloud.

You didn't flinch.
You listened.
Like every scar was part of the story.
Like the story still deserved a happy ending.

I remember you tracing my tattoo like you were reading it in braille.
Each line, each mark, you followed it with such care.
And when I began to tell you the meaning behind it, behind me, behind all of it,
you just listened.
Truly listened.
And in that stillness, I felt seen.
Like maybe I wasn't just a girl with stories.
Maybe I was worth reading.

I remember lying next to you once,
watching the way your chest rose and fell,
how the soft glow from the hallway touched your face like moonlight.
And I thought:
This. This is what safe feels like.

You once traced my spine with your fingertips,
like you were following a map.
And when I whispered that I was scared,
you didn't say, *"Don't be."*
You just pulled me closer.

Love with you wasn't fire.
It was warmth.
Not the kind that burns,

but the kind that lives in skin

and lingers long after touch.
The kind that curls up next to you and stays.

There were mornings I didn't want to leave the bed,
not because the world was too much,
but because being wrapped in you felt like being wrapped in a
sunrise.
And I wanted to stay in that light forever.

We made waffles once on a rainy Thursday.
The batter spilled everywhere,
you burned the first batch,
and we laughed so hard I forgot the sound of my own
overthinking.

That's what you gave me,
space to be silly,
to be soft,
to be someone I liked being.

You never needed me to perform happiness.
You created a life where it grew on its own.

When I told you about the things that hurt me,
not all at once, but in small, trembling fragments,
you didn't look away.
You held the story like it was delicate,
but not dangerous.
You didn't try to fix it.
You just made room for it.
And somehow, that was enough to start healing.

My mind, always so loud,
finally listened when your hand found my back.
Your touch was a quiet kind of reassurance,
a hush after the chaos.
A quiet room after years of noise.

With you, I didn't have to pretend.
I didn't have to shrink.
There was no need to armor myself with silence or strength.
I could just be,
soft, messy, vulnerable,
and still be held.

And I kept thinking:
Is this what love is supposed to feel like?
Like gravity?
Like belonging?

I told you once that I wanted to wake up next to you forever.
Not in a dramatic, fairytale way.
In the quiet, Tuesday-morning kind of way.
Where we make coffee half asleep.
Where your heartbeat pulls me back to reality.
And reality is good.
Because it's you.
It's us.

I don't remember the exact day I realized I was in love with
you.
But I remember the feeling.
It came in waves, soft, sure, constant.
It came in your forehead kisses.
Your sleepy voice whispering "good morning."
The way you never asked me to be anything other than ex-
actly who I was.

And isn't that love?
Not the explosion.
But the pull.
The staying.
The way the world shifts
until one person becomes your center.

That's what you were to me.
A quiet force, anchoring everything.
Not a star that burned out too fast,
but one that stayed.

★₀°☆ **Chapter 3: Orbit** ☆°₀★

"Not all love is a firework.
Some love is a quiet gravity,
two stars pulled into the same rhythm,
spinning soft and steady,
creating a home out of orbit."

We fell into rhythm before we even realized we were dancing.
No grand gestures.
No sweeping declarations.
Just a slow, steady unfolding.

It happened in the way your hand would find mine on the couch,
without asking, without looking.
In the way your hoodie ended up in my closet like it belonged there.
In the way I stopped checking the time
when I was with you.

We made a playlist together.
Not one of those perfect, curated ones,
it was messy, chaotic, us.
Some songs made me cry,
some made you laugh,
some we couldn't agree on,
but all of them felt like tiny pieces of home.

And every time I pressed play,
I felt you there.
Even when you weren't.

We watched movies together like it was a ritual.

Legs tangled.
Popcorn spilled between the sheets.
You always talked during the emotional parts,
and I always shushed you.
But truthfully?
I loved hearing your voice
cut through the silence.

You made space for me in everything.
On your couch.
In your playlists.
In your stories.

You'd tell me about the things you loved,
your favorite video games,
your childhood memories,
your music.
And I would just listen.

Because hearing you speak about something you cared about
was like listening to sunlight.
Like watching a star spin slowly,
letting its light stretch across a quiet sky.

And sometimes, in those moments,
I'd forget to breathe.
Not because I was overwhelmed,
but because I'd never felt so safe.

We drank coffee together in the mornings like it was holy.
Two mugs.
Two sleepy smiles.
No need for conversation.
Just warmth between us,
the kind that brewed slowly,

quietly.
The kind that filled a room without ever needing to be loud.

I'd watch you stir your cup like it was the most natural thing
in the world,
and I'd think,
How lucky am I to witness you like this?

Not the polished version.
Not the performative.
But you.
Real. Raw. Unfiltered.
And still, mine.

You made love feel like routine,
but never like a habit.
It didn't grow old.
It grew roots.

And I didn't need adventure.
I didn't need chaos.
I just needed the way you looked at me when I laughed too
hard.
The way you pulled me close when I got quiet.
The way your voice dropped when you said my name
like it was your favorite word.

We didn't have a fairytale.
But we had waffles and sleepy kisses.
We had matching coffee mugs
and movie nights that turned into morning.
We had shared toothbrushes,
half-watched TV shows,
and things that somehow ended up in each other's drawers.

We had a life.
And it was full of so much light.

You made me feel things I thought had died inside me.
Like joy.
Like softness.
Like being loved without fear.

You made me fall in love with writing happy poems again.
With ink that didn't ache.
With verses that laughed.
With metaphors that felt like sunshine.

And I started seeing everything through the lens of you,
you were the smile in my mornings,
the calm in my nights,
the orbit I kept choosing to stay in.

I remember one night,
you were talking about something you loved,
I can't even remember what it was now,
but your eyes lit up in a way that made my heart ache.

And I just watched you.
Listened.
Fell in love all over again.

That's what loving you felt like,
falling, over and over,
not because I had to,
but because you made me want to.

There were no fireworks.
No burning skies.
Just light.

Soft, constant light.

And I would've lived there forever,
in that stillness,
that sweetness,
that sacred orbit
we built with our hands.

⋆₀°☆ *Chapter 4: The Still Sky* ☆°₀⋆

"Sometimes, the sky is too quiet.
Too perfect.
Too still.
As if the world is holding its breath
before it breaks."

I didn't know it was the last time.

Not when I kissed you that morning.
Not when we laughed over coffee.
Not when you reached for my hand without thinking.
Everything felt the same, soft, steady, real.

We were on a trip together.
Just the two of us.
Waking up in unfamiliar sheets that still somehow felt like
home
because you were there beside me.

We walked through small towns,
pointed at houses we'd like to live in one day.
You said, "Imagine a dog running down that hallway."
And I smiled, because I already had.

There was a moment,
somewhere in between choosing snacks at the gas station
and arguing over which playlist to put on,
where I looked at you
and thought,
We're going to be okay.
We're building something.

We sat in the car,
and you rested your hand on my thigh like it belonged there.
And I believed you were staying.
I believed in us.

The way you spoke about next summer.
The plans we didn't write down but quietly promised each
other.
The way you kissed my forehead when I started to overthink,
none of it felt like goodbye.

That day was filled with so many small forever's.
And I clung to each one without even knowing I should.

We stopped for food.
You made fun of how I always order the same thing.
I rolled my eyes.
You kissed my cheek.
I laughed.

And it's only now,
replaying it all,
that I realize how carefully you were memorizing me.
Like you knew you were leaving,
but couldn't say it out loud.

Maybe that's the cruelest part,
that you still held me.
Still smiled.
Still looked at me like I was your future
just days before you took it all back.

You didn't give me a warning.
You gave me love.

You gave me closeness.
Softness.
Plans.

The last kiss didn't taste like ending.
It tasted like everything we hadn't finished.
Everything we thought we still had time for.

And I wonder now,
were you already slipping?
Were you already drifting?
Did something change inside you
while I was still falling deeper?

Or were you just scared?
Not of me.
But of how much this meant.
Of how real we had become.

I wish I could go back
to the stillness of that sky,
before I knew what silence was capable of.
Before the quiet became a warning
instead of comfort.

Because that was the day
you spoke to me like you were staying.
And I believed you.
I always did.

⋆₀°☆ **Chapter 5: Disappearance** ☆°₀⋆

"Some disappearances aren't loud.
They begin in love,
and end in nothing but air."

I read a quote once that said,
"I love you all ways. Always."
And when I read it,
I thought of you.

Because that's what it was with us, wasn't it?
Love in every form.
In the chaos.
In the calm.
In the quiet, where your hand found mine without needing to speak.
In the laughter that made my cheeks ache and my heart float.
In the silence where your presence said everything.

I loved you in all the ways
I never thought I could love someone,
and in all the ways
I never thought someone could love me.

All ways. Always.
That's what I told myself.
That's what I believed.

But maybe "always"
was only true for me.

I didn't understand how love could vanish like that.
Not ours.
Not the kind that had laughed only days before,

that had held hands under blankets,
planned meals,
shared futures in whispers.

There was no warning.
No betrayal.
No slow drifting.
Just... the shift.
The unraveling of everything soft,
without a sound.

It wasn't a storm.
It wasn't rage.
It was something worse,
something quieter.
A silent, brutal undoing.

You didn't raise your voice.
You didn't shut me out.
You didn't run.

You cried.

You cried harder than I've ever seen you cry.
And God, I wish you hadn't.
Because if you'd been cold, I could've hated you.
If you'd been indifferent, I could've let go.
But you stood there,
crumbling in front of me.

Your shoulders shook.
Your chest heaved.
You covered your face like the weight of it was too much,
like you wanted to disappear into your own hands.
And I just stood there,

frozen.

Watching the boy I loved break
right in front of me,
without reaching for me,
without trying to hold on.

And still,
you left.

I remember how you sat down,
how your voice cracked when you said,
"I don't know what I feel anymore."

Not I don't love you.
Not This isn't working.
Just I don't know.

As if confusion could explain
why my whole world was suddenly collapsing.

You said it had nothing to do with me.
That something in you had shifted.
That you didn't know when it happened,
or how,
or why.
That you didn't want to hurt me,
but couldn't lie to me either.

And I believed you.
Even as every word felt like a blade.
Even as I stood there with my heart in my hands,
begging for answers
without ever saying a word.

Because I didn't know what to say.
I didn't know how to fight for someone
who was already halfway out the door.

You cried,
and I held it.
Like I always did.
Like it was my job to catch your heartbreak
even while you were creating mine.

You apologized through tears.
You kept saying, "I'm sorry. I'm so sorry."
And I wanted to scream,
Then stay. Just stay.
But instead, I stayed silent.
Because I knew you wouldn't.

You broke us,
and I comforted you.

Because that's who I was to you, wasn't I?
Your safety.
Your softness.
Your shoulder to fall apart on,
even as you were walking away from me.

You leaned on the love you were leaving.
And I let you.

Because part of me thought maybe,
just maybe,
if I held you tightly enough,
if I stayed gentle enough,
you'd remember.
You'd change your mind.

You'd look at me and realize
what we were losing.

But you didn't.

Your tears didn't stop your silence.
Your sadness didn't rewrite the ending.

And that's what I'm still trying to live with.
Not just that you left,
but that it hurt you,
and you still chose to leave.

You knew it would break me.
You knew how fragile I was,
how deep I loved you,
how safe you were in my heart.
You knew.
And you did it anyway.

You cried for what you were leaving behind,
but not enough to stay.
You wept for the life we were losing,
but not enough to want it back.

And I…
I stood there,
watching you grieve the very thing
you were choosing to walk away from.

You shattered us
with trembling hands,
with red eyes,
with a goodbye you never even said aloud.

And somehow,
that made it worse.

Because if it had been cruel,
if you'd been cold,
I could've hated you.

But you were just as sad as me,
and still,
you let go.

⋆₀°☆ **Chapter 6: Dark Matter** ☆°₀⋆

"Some stars don't die in fire.
They vanish,
collapsing inward,
leaving behind only silence
and questions."

I keep trying to find the moment it shifted.

The second the ground started to give way beneath us.
But there's nothing.
Just light. Just love. Just laughter.
And then…
nothing.

You didn't fade.
You didn't break.
You disappeared.
And I've been chasing echoes ever since.

It's the kind of grief that doesn't scream.
It hums quietly beneath my skin,
like a memory that refuses to leave.
Like a question that can't be answered
because it was never asked out loud.

I don't understand.
And maybe that's what breaks me the most.
Because love, the kind we had,
it doesn't just stop.

It doesn't go from forehead kisses to silence overnight.
From I'll always be here to I'm not sure anymore
like it's just a change of plans.

And yet, here I am,
three weeks later,
looking at the same sky,
wondering how you can breathe so easily
while I'm still drowning in your name.

I think about the way you used to look at me.
The softness in your eyes.
The steadiness in your voice.
The way you said "Angi" like it meant something holy.

Were you lying?
Or did you change?

And what hurts more,
that I don't know you anymore,
or that maybe I never did?

You knew how much I feared being left.
You knew about the father who walked out,
the years I spent trying to be enough for people who never
stayed.
You knew how long it took me to trust someone again.
And still,
you left.

You didn't trip.
You didn't fall.
You walked.
Deliberately.
And closed the door behind you
like I was just another chapter you didn't want to finish read-
ing.

I wish I hated you.

Truly hated you.
But instead, I just miss you.
In the most infuriating ways.

I miss the way you looked at me while I talked about some-
thing I loved.
The way you'd pull me closer when I got quiet.
The sound of your voice at night,
when everything felt soft and certain and safe.

Now, even the quiet feels sharp.

The silence doesn't soothe.
It slices.

And the worst part?
I still don't have an answer.
No real reason.
Just the vague echo of "I'm not sure anymore."

How can you not be sure
of something that felt like home?

How can you not be sure
of someone who gave you every soft part of themselves
and asked for nothing but to be chosen?

You were my safe place.
And now, even my memories feel like betrayal.

I walk past our lamppost,
the one where we always said goodbye.
Same spot. Same quiet.
But this time, you didn't look back.
You didn't smile into our kiss.

You just… let go.

And now that corner feels haunted.
Not by your presence,
but by your absence.

It waits for you.
Even though I've stopped.

I hate that I still imagine you walking back to me.
That I still replay your laugh in my head
like a song I can't delete.

I hate that I counted your freckles the last time we met.
That I noticed the new ones.
That the sun finally came out after weeks of rain,
and I thought, Maybe that's a sign.

But the only sign you gave me was distance.
And now I wonder if the sun was shining for you,
or for the version of you I made up in my head.

Maybe I never really knew you.
Maybe I just loved the way you made me feel.

But how can that be true
when I still remember the way you held my face in your
hands
like I was something fragile and worth protecting?

You knew.
You knew what I carried.
You knew how much it took for me to trust you.
And you left anyway.

And I want to scream that.
To shake the universe until it gives me an answer.
But instead, I just whisper it into my pillow at night:
Why?
Why did you go?
Why didn't you stay?

You once told me you chose the wooden flowers because they
wouldn't wilt.
Because they'd last.

They're still on my shelf.
Still beautiful.
Still whole.

We're not.

Now they bloom in silence,
a reminder of the lie you didn't mean to tell,
that some things are meant to last.

Maybe you believed it, too.
Back then.

Maybe that's what makes this so impossible.
We both believed in forever.
You just stopped.

And I didn't.

And I still haven't.

Sometimes,
not often,
just on soft days,

I wish you'd come back.
Not to stay.
Just long enough
for me to count your freckles again.
All of them.
One more time.
Like maybe if I memorized them again,
you'd remember me too.

⋆₀°☆ **Chapter 7: Starlight Echoes** ☆°₀⋆

"Some stars are so far away
that we see their light long after they've burned out.
That's how love feels, sometimes,
bright, even in its absence."

I still love you.
Or maybe I just love the version of you that loved me.
The boy who made playlists for us.
The boy who kissed my forehead like it was something sacred.
The boy who spoke about the future like he actually meant it.

I don't know if that version of you ever really left,
or if he just slipped into another orbit,
out of reach but still burning in the distance.

Sometimes, I catch myself writing about you in the present tense.
As if part of me refuses to update the verb.
As if part of me still believes
you're just a phone call away,
just a heartbeat away,
just one brave moment away from coming home.

But you're not.

You're a light I can still see
even though the star has already gone dark.

I would have never done this to you.

I would have held your shaking hands.
I would have stayed through the fear,

the confusion,
the nights when love feels heavier than either of us knew how
to carry.

I would have built a home out of every kiss.
Would have fought for you,
even when you forgot how to fight for yourself.
I would have stayed.
Always.

Because that's what love is supposed to be.
Not easy.
Not perfect.
But certain.

And that's the part you never understood,
that real love doesn't walk away when it gets heavy.

It stands.
It stays.

Now, I tell myself
you don't deserve my words.

You don't deserve the poems I bleed at 2 a.m.
You don't deserve the pieces of me
I so willingly handed over,
thinking you'd keep them safe.

My love was stitched into every syllable.
Every line I wrote for you was a home.
A refuge.

And you,
you read my heart,

felt the weight of it,
and still turned away.

No more poems
for hands too unsure to catch them.

Next time,
my words will fall only into hands steady enough to hold
them.
Into hearts that will see my verses as treasure,
not burden.

But even still,
I find myself loving you in small, forbidden ways.

In the way I pass a coffee shop we once shared a morning in.
In the way I hear a song from our playlist and still smile
before the sadness can catch up.

I love you, sometimes,
without meaning to.
In the echoes.
In the soft spaces between healing and hurting.

And maybe that's okay.
Maybe that's all love ever becomes after it ends,
a memory with its own kind of gravity.
A starlight echo,
still beautiful,
even if it no longer leads anywhere.

You didn't deserve the kind of love I gave you.

You couldn't even hold it.

And still,
some part of me
will always hope you remember
what it felt like
to be loved like that.

Because love like mine
doesn't vanish.
It leaves starlight behind.
It leaves warmth in the places you'll visit alone.
It leaves poetry you'll never hear again.

You left.
But the love I gave you still flickers in the dark.
Not for you to return to.
Not for you to claim.
But as a quiet reminder,
I loved you right.

Even when you didn't know how to stay.

⋆₀°☆ **Chapter 8:**
The Light of Our Last Star ☆°₀⋆

"Some stars leave their light behind,
a warmth that lingers long after they're gone.
You were that for me.
And I am still shining."

I imagine it sometimes.

Not often,
not in a desperate way,
just in the quiet spaces,
in the soft folds of memory that I haven't unfolded in a while.

Walking down a busy street,
turning a corner,
and there you are.

Older, maybe.
Different in ways that would break my heart a little,
not because you changed,
but because I no longer know the map of you.

Your hair would be a little messier.
Your eyes a little heavier.
Your laugh maybe slower, like life taught you a few harder
lessons.

And for a moment,
the world would fall still.
Just like it did the first time we met.

Maybe you'd catch my eye first.

Maybe you'd stop mid-step,
uncertain whether to wave,
to smile,
to say anything at all.

Maybe I'd just stand there,
watching the years flicker between us,
feeling the weight of every unspoken word.

Not anger.
Not regret.
Just... tenderness.
The ache of something once holy
now belonging to the past.

And maybe, quietly,
you'd walk toward me.

We wouldn't need a script.
We wouldn't need to rehearse.
We were always better unscripted anyway.

You'd say my name,
softly.
Almost the way you used to,
but with a crack around the edges.

And I'd smile.
A real smile.
One that says: I'm okay now.

You'd ask how I've been.
I'd tell you the truth.
That I've learned to build a life around my own gravity.
That I write poems about the girl who stayed,

not the boy who left.
That I laugh louder now.
Sleep easier.

You'd nod,
looking down at your shoes,
trying to find the right words.

You might tell me you're proud of me.
That you knew I would find my way.
And for a moment,
I would want to believe you had always known that.

That even in your leaving,
there was a small part of you
that loved me enough to want me to grow.

I wouldn't ask you why you left.
Not anymore.

I wouldn't ask if you ever regretted it.
I wouldn't ask if you still dream about me sometimes,
in the quiet moments before sleep takes you.

Some questions are meant to stay unanswered.
Some love stories are meant to echo,
not return.

And I think...
I'd be okay with that.

Maybe you'd say you still remember the mornings we spent
tangled in sheets,
the way you used to hum songs we loved under your breath,
the way my coffee always tasted better than yours.

Maybe you'd say you still hear our playlist sometimes,
that a certain song plays and it pulls you back
to car rides, and laughter, and plans we once made.

Or maybe you wouldn't say any of it.
Maybe you'd just stand there,
in the space between apology and memory,
and let the silence say everything.

And I'd look at you,
and I'd see all the versions of you I once loved.

The boy who kissed me at the lamppost.
The boy who made me believe in soft mornings and long futures.
The boy who cried when he let me go.

And I'd realize, with a calm I didn't expect,
that I don't need you to come back.
Not anymore.

Because the love we had,
it didn't die.
It just changed forms.
It stretched itself into the stars,
into the poems,
into the girl who learned to keep shining
even when you couldn't stay.

You were **the light of our last star.**

And I'm no longer standing in the dark waiting for you.

I am standing in the light you left behind,
carrying it with me

into all the places you'll never see.

If I see you again,
I hope you'll see it,
the way I stayed kind.
The way I stayed soft.
The way I kept loving,
even when the world asked me not to.

I hope you'll know
you were loved by someone who would have stayed forever.

I hope you'll remember
that you once held the heart of a girl
who believed in stars,
in songs,
in love that didn't need to be loud to be lasting.

And I hope,
above all,
that you carry the memory of that love
like a quiet constellation
in the back of your mind.

Something good.
Something golden.
Something you don't find again.

Maybe you'll want to say more.
Maybe I will too.
But I think, instead,
we'll just smile one last time.

And then we'll keep walking.
You toward your future.

Me toward mine.

Under different skies.
Under the same stars.

Angelina Schreiber

To you,

To everything you were,
everything you are,
and everything you will be.

To the way you walked into my life
like a quiet sunrise,
slowly filling the spaces I thought
would always remain dark.

To the way your laughter felt like home,
your hands like an unspoken promise,
your love like the safest place I've ever known.

To the person you were before me,
to the person you were beside me,
to the person you will become,
I will always be cheering for you.

Always.

The Light of Our Last Star